Heart Chords

Harmony in a Soul Set Free

Reflections

Colossians 3:16

Lois Williams

xulon
PRESS

www.xulonpress.com

DEDICATION

To You, my Heavenly Father,
the Maker of Music,
the Creator of Harmony.
With these words
and the music in my soul,
I praise You.

CONTENTS

Acknowledgments

A collection of thoughts such as the contents of this book is a result of many years of prayer combined with the discipline of journaling. Through those years, there are many people to whom I owe my gratitude for their loving encouragement, support, and wise counsel. It would be impossible to name everyone who has come alongside and helped open my heart to receive. What blessed gifts they have offered with their affirmation! I thank all of you who have touched me with your comments of appreciation for the words I have shared in my poetry.

Specifically, though, I would like to mention a few.

Susan Muller, dear friend, who sees the struggles that aren't always pretty and who lifts me up with her special kind of heartening reassurance and cheer. Thank you for loving me.

I am grateful to Paul Pew, from whom I have learned so much about music, for his gifts of teaching and directing. It has been one of the joys of my life to sing under his leadership and to revel in his incredible compositions. Thank you for all your help in putting this book together, and your unfailing encouragement. You have blessed me.

Thank you, Lou Ann Miller, too, for your assistance in proofreading this manuscript and the many ways in which you encourage me.

And my amazing soul mate, my husband, Fred. What a gift you are to me! There aren't words to express the depth of my love for you and my thanks for the way you support me and stand quietly with me to be for me and do for me whatever I need. You are a wonderful husband, a true companion and a joy that fills my days.

Finally, my Heavenly Father. With gratitude for the gift He has poured over me with His incredible healing grace and mercy; for allowing me the wonder of words that have freed my soul and brought harmony into my heart.

"My heart is steadfast,
O God; I will sing
and make music with
all my soul."

Psalm 108:3 (NIV)

FOREWORD

I thank God for music. It is a solid illustration of His marvelous creative power. He lets our ears experience organized sound in a way that somehow magically touches our hearts. In so doing He awakens us to the harmony with which He desires to delight us. I have found over the years of His working in my life that there are many ways of connecting with Him. Each of the following must be included in our worship. From them comes the music that sets the believer free. **Longing**, coming to Him to fill the empty spaces. **Listening** to His voice and accepting that He listens to us. **Learning** that comes from His word, following His instructions, believing His promises. **Leaning** on Him means doing what He commanded, trusting and obeying. **Living** a life that is abundant, benefiting from the harmony that intimacy with Him brings. **Loving** Him and **loving** our neighbors encompass the greatest commandments, as Jesus emphasized. Because of all the above, **lauding** Him... praising Him with a full heart.

The meditations in this book are my praise offerings. It is to Him, my Creator, my Sustainer, the Maker of music in my soul, that all the glory and praise belongs. He is my song. He is worthy. Soli Deo Gloria!

Longing

"Oh, God, you are my God,
earnestly I seek you;
my soul thirsts for you,
my body longs for you,
in a dry and weary land
where there is no water."

Psalm 63:1 (NIV)

ACCEPTED IN THE BELOVED

"So it shall be on Aaron's forehead, that Aaron (the High Priest) may bear the iniquity of the holy things which the children of Israel hallow in all their holy gifts and it shall always be on his forehead that they may be accepted before the LORD." Exodus 28:38 (NKJV)

"...to the praise of the glory of His grace, by which He has made us accepted in the Beloved." Ephesians 1:6 (NKJV)

There's a longing in a soul
so deep it is seldom verbalized,
yet it motivates behavior and attitudes.
It is an urge to be accepted,
to be an acknowledged part of something
that defines and identifies and affirms
who we are.

That longing is a part of our created being,
placed by God to impel us to find our
completion in Him.
We try and try, however,
to find contentment everywhere else
until His whisper reaches the soul depths.
"You are Mine.
Your High Priest, Jesus Christ,
bearing your guilt upon Himself,
ensures that, in the Beloved;
in Him, my Son...
you are accepted."

FOUND!

"It was right that we should make merry and be glad,
for your brother was dead and is alive again,
and was lost and is found." Luke 15:32 (NKJV)

In order to be found
one must be lost.
In order to rejoice in being found,
one must know he is lost.
Being found is the result of a search;
a search that begins with the
desire in a heart to find.

I was the object of a search
and I didn't even know it,
not until I was found
by my loving Savior.
Now I rejoice,
because I know I *was* lost,
and the efforts to "find myself" are over.
I can never find my self
without first being found by Him.

ARID SEASON

"The desert and the parched land will be glad;
the wilderness will rejoice and blossom. Like the
crocus, it will burst into bloom; it will rejoice greatly
and shout for joy." Isaiah 35:1, 2 (NIV)

Cactus blooming!
From prickly dry exterior
the seemingly impossible occurs.
A flower appears,
its waxy brilliance a sharp
contrast with the dusty desert hues
that surround it.

I am amazed and encouraged
by what I see before me,
because I've felt dry, and prickly,
and it seems impossible
that there is any beauty
waiting to bloom in me.

Yet without seeing it, who would believe
a cactus could sprout a flower?
The God of miracles Who makes
the cactus bloom in its season
is well able to use my arid season
and bring forth the blossom of His love
for everyone to see in me.

THIRST

"He shall be like a tree planted by the rivers of water, that brings forth its fruit in its season; whose leaf also shall not wither; and whatever he does shall prosper."
Psalm 1:3 (NKJV)

My branches are dry,
demanding moisture.
It is so necessary for my growth.
I'm thirsty.
Without water I will dry up,
my green leaves will curl, drop off,
and the buds of forming fruit
will never be what they
were intended to be.
Ever deeper into the soil
I thrust my roots;
seeking, searching.
The scent of Living Water
attracts and,
desperate for life,
I press for the reservoir
and gulp...
sending the precious droplets
to every branch,
every leaf,
every bud.

I'm satisfied.

DROUGHT

"Come all you who are thirsty, come to the waters..."
Isaiah 55:1 (NIV)

Dusty automobiles,
dried-up lawns,
flowers wilting in the heat.
There's a water shortage.
The abundance to which
we've become accustomed
is suddenly rationed.
We are in a drought,
and it is irritating to feel ourselves deprived.
How wasteful I've been,
considering the supply endless.
Now, mourning the lack,
I am chagrined to realize
all I've taken for granted.

But what about my spiritual drought?

I can't complain about using up
the Living Water available to me;
its Source is unending.
Yet I don't partake from its fountain
nearly as freely as I have drawn from the faucet
of earthly water which is running dry.
I need both to survive.
But I must conserve the one and gulp the other.
How incredible to realize that
the water that fills my eternal spirit
flows unceasingly from the Fountain of life
and will never, ever
lead to a drought.

CRUMBS

"You shall eat in plenty and be satisfied, and praise the name of the LORD your God Who has dealt wondrously with you." Joel 2:26 (NJKV)

Crumbs fall my way
as I crouch beneath the table of the world.
Crumbs that tantalize,
yet leave me begging for more.
Crumbs of approval, of material things.
My mouth is accustomed to the
flavors of the old life...
tasting good, then turning bitter, demanding,
always demanding, more.
More to take away the dry acid taste
of flavors that never satisfy,
the leeks and garlic of the Egypt season in my life.
It should be no surprise to me,
but so often I am amazed at the emptiness
after a banquet of crumbs.

Somewhere I hear the call of
the Lord of Hosts announcing a feast.
Delectable, rich treats are offered,
to be enjoyed by all who choose to attend.
I'm invited. Everyone is.

So why do I sit here with hands extended,
existing on crumbs?
As flavorful as they may be
there is no comparison between crumbling fragments
and a full bite of satisfying richness.

TINY MORSELS

"Let them give thanks to the LORD for his unfailing love and his wonderful deeds for men, for he satisfies the thirsty and fills the hungry with good things." Psalm 107:8, 9 (NIV)

"Then the angel said to me, 'Write: "Blessed are those who are invited to the wedding supper of the Lamb!" Revelation 19:9 (NIV)

Pulling a pan of roasted chops from the oven,
I inhaled the delicious scent I'd been sniffing for hours.
I was hungry.

Stuck behind in the pan was a tiny morsel of stuffing,
a cube of bread soaked with juice and spices,
baked to a crisp.
Of course I ate it! It melted in my mouth.
So rich, so tasty, it made me hungrier for dinner.

I was thinking that I only get a taste of God here on earth,
a tiny morsel, compared with the richness ahead.
Each taste of Him makes me hungrier for more.

If each tiny morsel I have now brings me
such soul-filling joy, I can only imagine
what the wedding supper in heaven will be like!

DESSERT

*"But you would be fed with the finest of wheat; with honey
from the rock I would satisfy you." Psalm 81:16 (NIV)*

I am filled with the presence of God.
He has answered my prayer,
fed me with His word,
shown me His love and care.
Yes. I am full...

As from an "all-you-can-eat" buffet
I have sampled my way through all
that I could fit on my plate.
Yet, there is still the dessert table,
and as sated as I feel, I still want
the sweetness that awaits.

Full doesn't always mean filled.
Otherwise we would not be tempted
to have dessert!

So, God, I long for more of You.
I thank You for the banquet I've tasted,
but ask You to serve me
a big helping from Your dessert tray.
I want to be filled with the sweetness
of intimacy with You.

MOONLIGHT GOLD

*"I will give you the treasures of darkness, riches stored in
secret places, so that you may know that I am the LORD, the
God of Israel, who summons you by name." Isaiah 45:3 (NIV)*

Treasures of darkness.
I don't see treasures very often
when pain fills my days
and encompasses my nights,
though God promises them to me.
I have heard it said that
it is possible to gather gold,
where it may be had, by moonlight.

I guess it is true that
gold is visible in the dimmest
light if one but looks.
Its reflective nature doesn't need
the sun to bring forth its gleam.
Perhaps its beauty is more precious
if it is glimpsed in the pale glow
of moonlight than in the blaze of noonday sun.

And, so I think it is true that our faith,
triumphing in the dark night of trial and suffering,
shines with holy fire.
A transcendent shimmer that could not be seen
in the bright sunshine of seeming prosperity.
So many gems and precious metals
come from the deep parts of the earth;
treasures of darkness.

God, please make me shine for you
with the gold you are mining
by moonlight in my life.

CONSIDERING JOY

"Consider it pure joy, my brothers, whenever you face trials of many kinds; because you know the testing of your faith develops perseverance. Perseverance must finish its work so that you may be mature and complete, not lacking anything." James 1:2-4 (NIV)

"Let us fix our eyes on Jesus, the author and perfecter of our faith who for the joy set before Him, endured the cross...consider Him." Hebrews 12:2, 3 (NIV)

I'm staring heartache in the face...
seeing a painful road ahead.
And I'm certainly not eager
to embrace it and call it joy.
So it's with a bit of rebellion that
I recall this passage of scripture.
Pulled deeper into the words of God,
though, it tells me why.

I am to walk through the trial,
building a strengthening faith with each step;
and the joy that awaits,
though no doubt tinged with sorrow
when this particular trial has passed,
will be the contentment of a
new knowledge of a faithful God
whose sustaining presence along the road
lifts me to a higher level of completeness in Him.

It's difficult to quash
the rebelliousness of my humanity;
to open myself in anticipation
when dread stalks each moment,
but unless I do, I will never know
the reality of faith-infused joy.

Jesus walked a painful path, too,
for the joy that was set before Him.
So, considering Him...I'm ready for my path.
I will consider it joy.

THE THREEFOLD CORD

"...and a threefold cord is not quickly broken."
Ecclesiastes 4:12 (NKJV)

Dear God, inside me is a longing,
a demand for intimacy that, unmet,
cuts my heart in pieces.
You created that yearning, didn't You?
Was it when You knit me together
in my mother's womb?

I have tried to fill it, struggled to find completion;
but now I see in the mirror of my mind,
no earthly relationship was, nor will ever be, enough,
because my need is You.

You, my Father, desire to be my friend
in every beautiful sense of the word,
to fill the empty longing so that
I might be whole, and in being made whole in You,
will be able to love and be loved.

From the completeness that surrounds
my surrender to Your friendship, Father,
may I reach outward, cradling no more
inward self-indulgence, to find the third strand
that makes the threefold cord.

MY WILDERNESS

"So He Himself often withdrew into the wilderness and prayed." Luke 5:16 (NKJV)

A place apart,
surrounded by nothing,
away from everything
save my Source.

I seek it,
search it out,
soak in God's presence
then return
to my place in life
surrounded by peace,
a part of everything,
yet rested and restored

I WAIT

"...the land on which your feet have walked will be your inheritance and that of your children forever because you have followed the LORD my God wholeheartedly... Now give me this hill country that the LORD promised me that day." Joshua 14:9, 12 (NIV)

I wait,
because I must.
Hearing Your voice staying me, Father,
heeding Your upraised palm.
Sensing that the mighty hands that halt me
hold me,
bringing comfort to my wilderness
and strength for the weary days.

I see ahead the hill country I have walked,
and I claim Your promised victory,
the inheritance that is mine.
I have known the beauty of Your faithfulness
upon my mountain
and so,
I wait.

Listening

"I will listen to what
God the Lord will say;
he promises peace to his people,
his saints...but not let them
return to folly."

Psalm 85:8 (NIV)

MONOLOGUE

"Speak, Lord, for your servant is listening."
I Samuel 3:9 (NIV)

I'm listening, aren't I?
At least I'm trying to hear.

The story of the child Samuel
has always stirred me
and I wonder…am *I* hearing from God?
Or am I, as I suspect, listening only
to my dialogue with Him.
Come to think of it, perhaps
monologue is a more
accurate description!

I'm doing a lot of talking here, it seems.
I'm not plugging my ears
with my fingers
but I think my monologue
is drowning out
the soft voice of God,
and it must wind down
into silence so that I can truly say,
"Speak, Lord, I'm listening."

SPEAK, LORD

"God, do not keep silent. Do not be deaf, God; do not be idle. See how Your enemies make an uproar; those who hate You have acted arrogantly." Psalm 83:1-2 (HCSB)

Speak, Lord,
Your enemies clamor.
Their voices rise
and hammer
against our ears.

Speak, Lord,
Your enemies unite,
their forces rise
and vow to smite
Your people here.

Speak, Lord,
let your holy breath
quench wicked goals;
putting them to death,
stubble before the wind.

Speak, Lord,
let hearts be stirred.
Burn rebellion to dust;
Your almighty words
creating the fire.

Speak, Lord,
shout out your name;
and confused, troubled foes
will cower in shame
before you, O Most High.

DESOLATION

"...because you have not heard my words...I will take from them the voice of mirth, and the voice of gladness, the voice of the bridegroom, and the voice of the bride, the sound of the millstones and the light of the lamp. And this whole land shall be a desolation..." Jeremiah 25:8, 10-11 (NKJV)

It came to the Beautiful Land
when the Old Testament kingdoms
refused to obey the LORD...desolation.
No more mirth or gladness,
no reason for it;
no more wheat to grind for food,
the candle's light extinguished,
their liberty turned to slavery.
Darkness, sadness, uselessness, captivity;
the price of disobedience.

When I am taken captive by
the selfishness of my flesh,
my joy is diminished,
my service damaged;
the light of His love in my life
dims and I taste bitter regret,
the price of my disobedience.

Please, God, may I hear, and heed, Your words
that I never again allow into my life
the agony of desolation.

THE DEW

"I will be like the dew to Israel; he will blossom like a lily. Like a cedar of Lebanon he will send down his roots; his young shoots will grow. His splendor will be like an olive tree, his fragrance like a cedar of Lebanon.
Hosea 14:5, 6 (NIV)

I bring my words of confession
to You, my Father.
I have wandered away, seeking selfish goals,
constructing idols with my own hands.
I come for Your refreshment,
promised as the early morning dew
sparkling like crystal in the sunlight.

What a beautiful picture
You've given me of Yourself, in the dew.
Shimmering, nourishing, life-giving;
it is Your presence of which You speak.

Let it cover me this morning,
encouraging the deepening of my roots,
strengthening the growth of the shoots
until my life is like the spreading olive tree,
reaching out to others,
and the fragrance of You
emanates from me as sweet as cedar.

DREAM SPINNER

*"My bones were not hidden from You when I was made in
secret, when I was formed in the depths of the earth. Your
eyes saw me when I was formless; all my days were written
in Your book and planned before a single one of them
began." Psalm 139:15-16 (HCSB)*

Where did my dreams begin?
Spun by God, as His breath
created my soul,
He placed them in the depths of my spirit.
Knitting me together,
He forged the longings, desires,
hope and imagination
into the creative core
that propels, moves, shapes,
and determines my path.

In the place God knows so well...
my very secret self
where conscious thought
so seldom flees...
yearnings conceive life plans
and I'm learning that
allowing Him to be my God
will grant the dreams
He's spun for me
and carry me to fulfillment
on wings of His spirit.

CAIN, ABLE?

"Then the LORD said to Cain, 'Why are you angry? Why is your face downcast? If you do what is right, will you not be accepted? But if you do not do what is right, sin is crouching at your door; it desires to have you, but you must master it'." Genesis 4:6-7 (NIV)

I read of Cain's sin, his rebellious sacrifice,
one that was unacceptable to God.
Refusing God's offer of a chance
to repent, to do it right, he compounded his sin,
and ignoring the warning from God
of a devouring enemy crouching outside his door,
committed the unthinkable, and
Abel's blood cried out from the ground.

I set myself up with pride,
never realizing that sin crouches
at the door of my disobedience.
Father, You come with outstretched arms
to ask if I am willing to bring another offering,
one of obedience.
I am able to do what's right, but I have a choice,
rebellion or compliance.

How often have I opened that door and
allowed the crouching enemy in?
Doing it my way brings only alienation,
a mark of despair upon my forehead.
Father, I repent. Please accept my confession;
forgive me as I turn away from the crouched serpent.
Receive my humble offering, the one I am able to bring
because of the sacrifice of Jesus.

RECOGNITION

"Wash me thoroughly from my iniquity, and cleanse me from my sin. For I acknowledge my transgressions, and my sin is always before me." Psalm 51:2-3 (NKJV)

I noticed a transgression, or two, today.
Sensed a displeasing attitude,
rebelled against my God's
clearly-spoken instructions.
He brought it to my attention
and I saw it for what it was...sin in my life.
So I waved at it in recognition.

It occurred to me this is what I often do.
Somewhat like seeing an acquaintance,
perhaps at the grocery store, and I wave in recognition.
If I desire to engage in conversation
I will stop and make the effort to connect.
But many times I'm guilty of ducking around a corner
to avoid an acknowledgement.
Perhaps I'm in a hurry, perhaps I look a mess,
perhaps I'm uncomfortable with that person.
Perhaps there's strife between us.
So I wave in recognition and move on
without truly acknowledging that presence.

God wants me to acknowledge my sin.
He knows there is no cleaning up,
no changing, in me until I do.
Am I in too much of a rush to meet with Him?
Am I ashamed of the mess I'm in?
Am I uncomfortable because of the strife
between us, due to my disobedience?
Am I waving and ducking to keep from engaging with Him?

Forgive me, Father, for I have sinned.

MY NAME IN VAIN

"You shall not take the name of the Lord your God in vain, for the LORD will not hold him guiltless who takes His name in vain." Exodus 20:7 (KJV)

I have become a victim.
A thief has stolen my identity
and has taken with it
my feelings of safety and invincibility.
And now I am struggling to make real
in my heart the truth that my safety is
in God's hands;
to find the promised peace
in spite of what has occurred.

How violated I feel to think that
someone is using my name, my credentials,
my reputation, nefariously; how insulted and angry I am.
My human heart wants revenge right now, not peace.

But the still, small Voice I am coming
to recognize whispers in my soul
and I am brought up short to
think how He must shudder at the
skewed use of His Name; the cursing,
the false prophets who litter the world's stage;
using the majestic Name of the Most High to
benefit themselves, defaming Him.

One day God will triumph, avenging His Name,
and He will wreak vengeance on my behalf
because I am His child.
'Til then, I must rest in His provision,
garnering strength from the everlasting Source
to deal with the myriad details of
clearing my name, without tarnishing His.

PERFECT HEARING

*"For the eyes of the Lord are on the righteous and His ears
are attentive to their prayer."*
Psalm 34:15 (KJV)

Father, I praise You
for your ever-listening ear.
I know it is attuned to my cry.
You hear me even when I'm not
totally aware that I'm crying out
because Your ear hears much more
than my words...
You hear the argument
between the flesh and spirit,
the desire to trust
embattled by the earthly need for control.
You hear the excuses, the protests;
You feel the hurt of my begging for Your help
accompanied by my pushing You away.
Yet Your ear never shuts against me.
(You promised!)
You never put in ear-plugs.
You hear and experience the whole battle,
so how sweet to your attentive ear
must be my words at long last,
"I surrender. I will trust You."

Father, help me learn to listen!

THE CALLING

"For the Word of God is living and powerful and sharper
than any two-edged sword, piercing even to the division of
soul and spirit and of joints and marrow, and is a discerner
of the thoughts and intents of the heart."
Hebrews 4:12 (NKJV)

Your piercing Word, Father...
I used to be so afraid of it
because my deeds didn't bear scrutiny,
particularly Yours.
I was running from You...
knowing I was running and too stubborn to return.
I feared the judgment of Your Word,
fleeing as a criminal pursued by the law.

But in my homecoming I
ponder this verse with sweeter clarity.
Your Word pierces to the place where
I really live in relationship with You,
my soul, my spirit. Are they Yours?
Or am I living life on my own terms?
Somehow, there's a difference now.
Instead of blinding panic and a desire to hide,
there arises within me a sense of poignancy,
a questioning, not of my deeds,
but of how I am doing with You.

Do I love You, Lord, really love You?
Only You know...
I want to know, too, in the depths of my soul.
I hear Your heart much louder and clearer
than the gavel of judgment upon me.
I won't run from You anymore.

Learning

"Show me your ways, O LORD,
teach me your paths; guide me
in your truth and teach me,
for you are God my Savior, and
my hope is in you all day long."

Psalm 25:4,5 (NIV)

TRAVEL PLANS

"Seek ye first the kingdom of God and His righteousness
and all these things will be added unto you."
Matthew 6:33 (KJV)

I'm headed out upon a journey.
It's a new commitment to God
to walk with Him;
a journey which I am concerned
about my ability to complete.
So I load my suitcase with carefully set-out goals,
well-laid plans, celebrated achievements,
and march purposely, fervently into the presence of God.
With a satisfied thud I lay the suitcase
down and invite Him to come along on my proposed
journey,
never suspecting that He might have
something else in mind!

I am bathed in chagrin as He dumps
my suitcase. The contents look
pitifully inadequate when stacked
against the bounteous provision He offers.
When will I learn to bring an empty suitcase
into the throne room of His majesty...
an eager soul in need of filling?
When will I cease to load my thoughts
with plans that I will never need?

God, please open my eyes to the vista
of the next step You have planned.
I'd rather simply hold Your hand
than lug my heavy suitcase down the road.

THE DAWN

*"The path of the righteous is like the first gleam of dawn,
shining ever brighter till the full light of day."*
Proverbs 4:18 (NIV)

What is lovelier than dawn,
the pearly purity of first light?

It is not yet day, but I sense its coming,
the ever-so-faint lifting of the darkness.
I have wakened early with a sweet anticipation,
not knowing why;
but as I sit here, I'm hearing Your voice, O God,
whispering in my heart.
Did You stir me from sleep for this reason...
to teach me, to show me Yourself?

Here in burgeoning daybreak
I wonder if this is not the way we come to know You.
Sitting in darkness (sometimes even when we *think*
we understand all about You) the light begins to appear.
Moment by moment, scripture by scripture,
experience by experience, You roll back the curtain.
The light gets brighter as dawn approaches,
and some day we will know Your true brilliance
the way we now see the noonday sun.

I am here in the pre-dawn, sensing the wonder;
excited, anticipating what is ahead as You open Yourself
    to me.
My spirit swells the way my earthiness responds
to this brightening day; not quite morning yet, but it's
    coming!

Father, how beautiful to greet the day with
your smile creating the dawn in my heart.

WATERFALL

"Have mercy on me, O God, according to your unfailing love; according to your great compassion blot out my transgressions. Wash away all my iniquity and cleanse me from my sin." Psalm 51:1-2 (NIV)

I'm thinking today, Lord Jesus,
about Your cleansing presence.
I read that phrase and it grabs my heart.
It is Your presence that cleanses
simply by being there.
You are the Living Water.
Your indwelling Spirit washes me constantly
as a waterfall cascades over stones,
flushing out soil and impediments,
gaining strength, and in its flow,
tosses crystal rainbows into the air.

Oh, to be ever cleansed by Your presence;
eroding my sinfulness,
reshaping the rocks of my old nature
with the waterfall of You.
I want my life to show only
the sparkling splashes of joy,
the proof of Your flowing in my life.
Will You do this for me?
Yes. I know You will.
So, I surrender.

THE MOUNTAIN

"Draw near to God, and He will draw near to you."
James 4:8 (NKJV)

The mountain appears suddenly
in the distance,
cone-shaped, magnificent.
I gasp in wonder and gaze steadily
as we approach.
Its proportions change
with the miles and miles we drive
bringing us close.
The nearer we come,
the more aware of its majesty we are.
Contours soften into snow-packed slopes;
jutting rocks depict contrasting edges.
We see so much more than we could at a distance.
It is no longer a remote peak
but a surrounding presence
and our senses are pulled into its beauty.

I think sometimes that's how I am with God.
He seems far away; magnificent, yes,
but distant, remote, far off.
When I draw nearer to Him, however,
my perception of Him changes.
I can see the softened slopes of His
mercy and grace and the jutting strength
of His promised faithfulness.
He has not changed, He will not change.
It is I who have come near;
seeing so much more than when
I viewed Him from afar;
and I am pulled into the beauty
of His surrounding presence.

WOUNDS

"He heals the brokenhearted and binds up their wounds."
Psalm 147:3 (NIV)

The idea of God's grace,
flowing over my flaws,
filters into my consciousness,
drawing my attention.
It awakens my heart to His revelation
that I've been presenting
Him with scars to heal;
scars that have already grown
over festering sores…
scars produced through
my meager efforts to heal myself.

Reluctant to open my broken spirit
for Him to touch the hurt,
I've never allowed that grace,
that mercy and love, to penetrate,
and cleanse the open wound.
It still throbs with pain
beneath the grown-over skin.

Is my awareness a sign
that I'm reaching a new place,
a place of willingness
to allow Him to lay open the scar,
flood my wounds,
and truly heal my soul?

MIRROR, MIRROR

"Now we see but a poor reflection as in a mirror; then we shall see face to face. Now I know in part; then I shall know fully, even as I am fully known." 1Corinthians 13:12 (NIV)

I pinch my cheeks to bring color
to my face and gaze at my reflection
in the mirror.
I wonder why I so often find
only ugliness when I look inside.
I see the misshapen warts of pride and envy,
the dark circles of disobedience under my eyes.

I hear that You see beauty in me, Father,
and I wonder how.
But then, Your mirror is different from mine.
Your eyes see me through Your
creative process...knowing what
is real and what is imaginary,
what you are making of me.
I look and see the evil queen;
You look through Jesus' blood
and see...Snow White.

Will you help me to reflect somehow to others
what You see in me in the mirror of Your heart?

SCARS

"But he was pierced for our transgressions, he was crushed
for our iniquities; the punishment that brought us peace
was upon him, and by his wounds we are healed."
Isaiah 53:5 (NIV)

The doctor said if I would trust him with my care
he could relieve my pain, perhaps even take it away.
I should be leaping with delight.
Instead I lie here swallowing panic.
I wonder why?

Could it be that I love my pain?
Is it possible that it has become such a
familiar companion that I dare not let it go
lest I no longer have it to define me?
Have I used my pain as an excuse?
I think, though, that there is fear in
trusting the doctor;
what if my hope is high and it doesn't work?
So here I lie, indecisive.

And I wonder about the pain of sin in my life.
Hurt, anguish, betrayal, disappointment,
and physical, chronic pain,
to which I cling in spite of myself.
The reality is that I'm emphasizing the scars
from my wounds, afraid to apply the
soothing balm that would heal my soul.
What would it be like to live pain free?

continued

And what will it be like to live sin free?
I will know that actuality someday.
Until then, however, I will carry scars,
Physical, emotional, spiritual scars.

Jesus, You died to heal my wounds.
If I accept Your healing work,
will You take my scars and turn them into
beauty marks?

THORNS

*"Cursed is the ground because of you; through painful toil
you will eat of it all the days of your life. It will produce
thorns and thistles for you..." Genesis 3:17-18 (NIV)*

Thorns and thistles in the ground,
a curse to plague Adam as he was cast out,
separated by his sin, from the Holy Presence.

*"Abraham looked up and there in a thicket he saw a ram
caught by its horns." Genesis 21:13 (NIV)*

Thorns caught the ram
on the mount as Abraham,
poised to strike the mortal blow upon his son,
was halted by an angel voice.

*"They stripped him and put a scarlet robe on him, and then
twisted together a crown of thorns and set it on his head."
Matthew 27:28-29a (NIV)*

Thorns pierced my Savior's brow
as He hung, cursed, upon a tree,
made sin, for me.
Drops of precious blood fell upon cursed ground;
its affliction reversed, and I, too, am redeemed.

THE DECREASING "I"

"He must increase, but I must decrease."
John 3:30 (NKJV)

An odd thing, really, spiritual growth.
Against all human logic,
growing strong spiritually
means the "I" (my ego)
goes from all caps to lowercase.
The smaller it gets,
the larger my capacity
for abundant living.

Upon the pages of my story
"GOD" must be in uppercase,
all caps, and more and more each day
the "i" reduced to lowercase.
I am coming to understand
that a shriveling "I"
gives space to a blossoming faith.

It's a fact. And I must make myself shrink,
so more and more of Him can be seen.

DOUBT

*"Come unto Me, all you who labor and are heavy laden
and I will give you rest." Matthew 11:28 (KJV)*

Doubt is a lonely place to be.
The intimacy, which had begun to feel familiar,
is fading as I turn my face from Yours
with a gnawing suspiciousness
that You are not sufficient
for what I think I need.

It's dark inside of doubt.
Not a place where You can be;
a cold setting for my distrust, my sin.
I don't like it here.
I feel lost, fear-ridden, and, yes, lonely.
Why do I stay?

Your beckoning, light-filled presence
awaits my repentance;
holding out arms of welcoming grace.
My steps are leaden, weighted
with the pull of earthly desire.
Yet I feel a stronger pull throbbing
within the center of my soul.
Your voice calls, "Come unto Me all you who labor…"
Such struggle, such labor—it should not be so.

Lifting my feet I head back toward the place we were.
One step of obedient trust and
there You wait, my Father, my Friend…
warmth and light and tenderness
shattering as with a laser beam
the loneliness of doubt.

NEWBORN

"Jesus answered and said to him, 'most assuredly, I say to you, unless one is born again, he cannot see the kingdom of God.'" John 3:3 (NKJV)

The other day I held an infant in my arms,
stroked the tender skin,
delighted in the dimpled flesh,
kissed the sweet spot behind the ear,
smelled the freshness of new life,
and exulted in the promise I was holding.

I was praising God for this tiny miracle,
thinking of all that lay ahead...
the first step, the first word
the thousands of other "firsts" that await...
and it seems that we lose our freshness so very easily.
Why am I not as thrilled to be able to walk
as this little one will be when he first
moves across the room on his own?
Why is not the joy of eating delicious food for me
as exciting as the first taste at his mother's breast
is for this small newborn?
Our eyes, our senses, become jaded and
we take for granted the marvelous gifts
of God that daily surround us.

So I am convinced that, in my spirit,
I am taking for granted the fact that
I have new life and am casually
walking along the way I always have,
because that's the way I learned it;
rather than depending on the Spirit
within me for renewal;
for the freshness, sweetness and
tenderness of a newborn, with which to see
the kingdom of God.

PERCEPTION

"Be self-controlled and alert. Your enemy the devil prowls around like a roaring lion looking for someone to devour. Resist him, standing firm in the faith..." I Peter 5:8, 9 (NIV)

Strange how our perception alters
in the presence of danger;
what in summer is an unnoticed
incline on the familiar road home
becomes an insurmountable hill when
coated with a sheet of ice.
Panic heightens our awareness:
causing us to look around for an escape,
wondering, what if....

Inching my way around a snow-packed curve
I was thinking of the need
for awareness of danger to my spirit;
learning to be watchful, not blithely heedless.
The enemy lurks in the familiar, the routine,
the complacency in which I operate
and can turn my life into a frightening slide
if I am not attentive.

I must watch the road with my Savior's eyes
and grip the wheel of grace tightly so that
He steers my course straight and true—
and keeps me out of the ditch!

POWER

"He (Christ) is not weak in dealing with you, but is
powerful among you. For to be sure, he was crucified in
weakness yet he lives by God's power. Likewise we are
weak in him, yet by God's power we will live with him to
serve you." 2 Corinthians 13:3b, 4 (NIV)

As I sit contemplating the difficulty
I'm having, living a life of victory,
I'm mesmerized by the tree outside my window
in the midst of a windstorm.
A new young tree that
I have watched from its beginnings.
Each spring it is larger, taller, fuller.
But today it is under attack by the wind.
Gust after gust bends the trunk far to the right,
yet during each pause in the onslaught
it rights itself.

What keeps it rebounding to erectness?

It is the life in the tree,
vibrant, strong and healthy,
powerful enough to bring the tree
upright again.

continued

And I am coming to realize,
there is a power that I often fail to recognize...
resurrection power...in me;
and even though I might be bowed and bent
by the tempting winds of old habits and comforts,
this resurrection power rests in me,
to enable, strengthen, remind
that I am to reckon myself dead to sin.
It can no more control me, that old life;
cannot break me, nor throw me to the ground.
My soul is alive through Jesus' resurrection,
He will stand me upright...
with the power of His life in me.

OBSTRUCTION

"For it is God who works in you to will and to act
according to his good purpose."
Philippians 2:13 (NIV)

A log in the river...
a victim, perhaps, of a huge storm,
laid flat with its roots to the sky,
settled deeply into the bed of the stream.
The river, undeterred, flows on,
its only concession is the pattern of ripples
the obstruction causes.

The river of God's love and grace flows
steadily around all the obstacles that
life's storms toss down in my path.
Sometimes the obstruction is so large
that it cannot be moved;
sometimes I despair in my struggle
to move past it.

But through the murmur of the water
here on the riverbank,
I hear God's whisper,
the reminder of His constancy,
and I see anew the lovely lacy froth of
bubbling ripples that is only made so
because of the obstruction.

And I thank Him for this beauty that
only He can cause to happen.

THE PATTERN

*"This is why Moses was warned when he was about to
build the Tabernacle. 'See to it that you make everything
according to the pattern shown you on the mountain."
Hebrews 8:5 (NIV)*

*"Let us fix our eyes on Jesus, the author and perfecter of
our faith..." Hebrews 12:2 (NIV)*

The wilderness Tabernacle...
a hallowed place of worship
built by God's children
according to the pattern
given to Moses on the holy mountain.

Related in scripture to us who are
God's children too, it is shown
as a picture of His Son Who
would Himself be our Tabernacle
through the redemptive act of His sacrifice.

Each detail of that tabernacle, no accident,
is personified in the Savior.
He's the door, the sacrifice on the altar,
His blood the cleansing power.
He's the Bread, the Light,
the sweet incense of intercession.
His flesh the torn and shredded veil,
His the glory that fills the holy of holies.
He's everything we need to enable our worship.

I am thinking that, just as Moses built
the earthly tabernacle according to the Heavenly pattern,
so we should be building our lives
according to the pattern laid out for us in Jesus.
Shouldn't we?

LIKE MOTHER, LIKE FATHER

*"And just as we have borne the likeness of the earthly man,
so shall we bear the likeness of the man from heaven."*
1 Corinthians 15:49 (NIV)

I wanted to be just like my mother.
I lost her when I was so very young.
Still, I thought I must replace her...
tried so hard, but the pattern was gone.
And I felt adrift most of my life.

Then one day someone said to me,
"You're just like your mother. It is déjà vu."
Thrilled to the core of my being, I wept.
Perhaps it's only the physical reminders
of her that I bear,
but something healed inside me
when I heard those words.

Remembering, I ponder the scripture
and think that I should be looking for signs
of growth, of working toward
being like You, Father.
Then it wouldn't matter if I had succeeded
in being like my mother.
I would be,
because she was like You!

THE CLOSET

"Therefore, we also, since we are surrounded by so great a cloud of witnesses, let us lay aside every weight, and the sin which so easily ensnares us, and let us run with endurance the race that is set before us." Hebrews 12:1 (NKJV)

Crammed with items
old and worn; convenient
for dumping unnecessary things I can't give up...
my closet.

Crammed with old fears,
guilt, hurts;
convenient for dumping problems
I've been unable to handle...
my life.

Disarray and undone tasks
rob me of useful space.
Yet daily plans to clean the closet
by evening find it cluttered still,
with more junk thrust inside.

Give me courage, Lord,
and energy
to untangle possessions,
to sort through worthless objects,
to recycle and discard.

And I will give you permission
to do the same in my life.
Oh, what a process it's going to be
cleaning out that closet...
and me.

GUARD MY WORDS

*"That which has gone from your lips you shall keep
and perform, for you voluntarily vowed to the LORD
your God what you have promised with your mouth."*
Deuteronomy 23:23 (NKJV)

I broke a promise today.
I caused pain,
and now I am filled with regret, and sorrow.
Oh, I know I can ask for forgiveness,
and no doubt receive it, from my loved one,
but I am realizing that
all the glue in the world
can not put back together
a promise that is shattered.

I guess that's why God takes
promises so seriously.
He never breaks His.
I think of all the times I have
promised Him something
and casually walked away,
my broken vows
trailing behind me.

The sickness I feel in the pit of my stomach now
is nothing compared to the ache in my soul
as I begin to comprehend how disappointed
He must be when I don't set a guard on my tongue
and carefully consider the words I say.
Because He loves me, He forgives me
when I repent, but a broken promise cannot be mended.

We just have to start all over again.

THE RESCUE
After the Earthquake

*"In my distress I called to the LORD; I cried to my God
for help. From his temple he heard my voice...He reached
down from on high and took hold of me; He drew me out of
deep waters...He brought me out to a spacious place; he
rescued me because he delighted in me."*
Psalm 18: 6, 16, 19 (NIV)

As I watch the awful pictures
of attempted rescue on my screen,
my heart is wrenched by the
nearly fruitless search for life.
But hope refuses to die and damaged, broken hands
frantically pull at stones; eyes blinded with tears and sweat
peer into instant graves, straining to see a movement;
ears are cocked to hear the faintest cry.

I was thinking of another rescuer, my Savior,
Who searched through the pile of stones
I had fallen under; rubble from the tower
of rebellion I'd been building, whitewashed by good deeds,
that tumbled down around me when the
earth quaked beneath that shaky structure.

A scene is burned in my mind forever;
a rescuer gently extricating a child from the rubble
and tenderly carrying her in his arms, rejoicing...
she lived!

O, Jesus, thank you for searching for me;
for digging with Your wounded, nail-scarred hands
until You heard the faint cry of my heart;
for carrying me in Your arms,
and fanning the spark of life into flame.

COTTON CANDY

"For all have sinned, and fall short of the glory of God."
Romans 3:23 (NKJV)

Do I see my sin?
Do I see myself as a sinner?
The question challenges me.

Sometimes I have seen the thoughts
that lurk beneath the levels of consciousness
where I live my life,
and I have acknowledged those thoughts.
But for the most part I think I consider
myself as pretty nice.
Any mention of sin usually elicits
a recitation of my good deeds;
and so I am aware this morning
that I have an incredible amount of
sugarcoating spinning around in the
whirling center of my mind, ready to
build a big cone of cotton candy to sweeten
the taste and appearance of my sinfulness,
and offer it to God for a bite.
It is a bad taste in His mouth.
He wants only my repentant heart,
confessing, throwing my sin on His altar.
Will I allow that brokenness
to be humbly laid at His feet?
For the sake of my healing,
God, please forgive my apathy,
my blind complacency.
I am a sinner.

DESIRES

"Blessed are those who hunger and thirst for righteousness, for they shall be filled." Matthew 5:6 (NKJV)

She wanted the toy reindeer,
her cheek pressed to its soft furry side,
her eyes big, pleading, blue pools of longing.
I hated to tell her "no", but she must learn...
none of us can have everything we desire.

I know exactly how she feels,
my expression no doubt as lustful as hers,
when yesterday I hugged
a soft green sweater to my own cheek;
arguing practicality with desire,
nearly as convinced of the necessity
of the addition of the sweater to my closet
as the importance to her of adding
a singing Rudolph to her toy chest.

I put the sweater down.
I did not buy the reindeer either.

So, God, today I wonder about
the true desires of my heart.
In my supposed maturity I comprehend
the difference between want and need,
but the intense yearning for things
too often surpasses my yearning for You.
Please take hold of my heart, Father.
May I look at You with pleading eyes,
hungering and thirsting for the
righteousness that truly fills my soul.

CHASTENING

"My child, do not make light of the Lord's discipline, and
do not lose heart when he rebukes you because the Lord
disciplines those he loves..." Hebrews 12:5, 6 (NIV)

The little child had misbehaved,
touched something not allowed,
grabbed in selfishness and caused distress.
I watched as her mother smacked her hands
to redirect her attention.
Startled, the child looked into her mother's face...
For correction? For direction? Questioning?
Her face crumpled in tears.

I turned away to hide my rueful smile,
remembering my young mother days,
but my smile faded soon as
I became aware that my
own hands had reached out and touched
things not pleasing to God;
that I had grabbed at my life
in my own puny strength
instead of accessing the Spirit's power
He has placed at my disposal.

I felt my hands being smacked.
And so I turn to look into His face...
there to see His compassion, His patience,
His desire for me to do what is right.
I am rebuked. And I know it.
But I see the love in His eyes, and,
chastened, ask Him to redirect my life.

CARRIED

"In all their distresses he too was distressed, and the angel of his presence saved them. In his love and mercy he redeemed them, he lifted them up and carried them all the days of old." Isaiah 63:9 (NIV)

I spent a lot of time trying to run away...
my own Israelite years...
and so, when I read these verses,
my heart lifts in joy,
even as I hang my head in
repentant sorrow.

I am coming to realize
that even now, my tendency
is to wander away
and I need to be reproved,
rescued from myself.

But then, what I find is that
I am still in my Father's arms,
carried by His love and mercy,
nearer than my next breath,
never distant,
and my heart swells in gratitude.

Thank You, God, for lifting me,
though heavy with rebellion;
carrying me,
never, ever, letting go.

SNOWFALL

"Through the LORD's mercies we are not consumed,
because His compassions fail not. They are new every
morning; great is Your faithfulness. 'The LORD is my
portion,' says my soul, 'therefore I hope in Him.'"
Lamentations 3:22-24 (NKJV)

As I stare out of the window,
I see the snow falling.
A part of me feels afraid, threatened, somehow,
and unsettled by plans that need to be changed.
Schedules must be altered because
life beats a different cadence to match the
slowing rhythm that a big snowfall brings.
Yet how lovely it is...
the white blanket that softens
jagged edges
and harsh angles.

I am thinking of Your faithfulness to me, God,
through all the seasons of my life,
now that my winter approaches.
And I feel a bit unsettled because
of changes that are coming.
Plans will be altered...
my dreams must adjust to
the new rhythm of my days,
for I can no longer accomplish
all the tasks I used to do.

continued

But with my winter, I hope,
will come a richer covering
of Your grace to blanket me
and soften the rough edges;
smooth the harsh angles of impetuosity
with Your wisdom
and deepen the beauty of Your life in me.
Because I know that
as surely as spring will follow,
(it always does, for You are faithful)
the end of my winter
will open the door to Spring eternal.

Leaning

"Trust in the LORD with all
your heart and lean not on
your own understanding. In all
your ways acknowledge him, and
he will make your paths straight."

Proverbs 3:5, 6 (NIV)

THE VINE LIFE I.V.

"Abide in Me..." John 15:4 (NKJV)

What does it mean to abide?
I read the definition...
"remain, stand fast, go on being"...
but what does it mean to me?
Especially in my relationship to God?
The scripture says we are to abide in Him,
in the Vine; that we can do nothing
without the mutual abiding...
I in Him, He in me.
I trust that He dwells in me,
but I seem to have some difficulty
understanding how I stay attached to Him.

Maybe it's sort of like an I.V.
At least that's how I am imagining it.
Whenever we are dehydrated,
whenever we are unable to eat on our own,
whenever we are in need of medicine,
the common practice is to hook up an I.V.
As long as we stay connected,
we receive the life-saving, life-giving necessity.

Not long ago I received a photo from my friend
taken during her chemo treatment.
Wrapped in a warm prayer shawl,
feet in warm fuzzy socks, she was resting, waiting,
and always trusting, that what she's receiving
via the I.V. will bring about her healing.

continued

That's what abiding is to me. I finally see.
This is how I can wrap my mind around
staying connected to God.
As the I.V. hooks the patient to a
constant flow of nutrition, or medicine,
or fluids; whatever the crisis demands,
so it must be with me.
Trusting that what I'm receiving is
exactly what I need, I will try never to
unhook my I.V. from the True Vine.

THE LIFE ABUNDANT

*"These things have I spoken unto you, that My joy might
remain in you, and that your joy might be full".*
John 15:11 (NKJV)

Satisfied by joy!
Abiding in Jesus, the True Vine,
is the condition for bubbling joy.
Thrills, giddiness, and happiness,
all come and go,
but contentment is painted on
by faith's brush strokes when joy is
allowed free rein.
Joy is the result of our choice to
stay rooted in the Vine.
Being cast off as a withered branch,
is the result of trying to bear fruit
on our own.

Removed from the joy,
the soul withers;
filled with the joy
the soul flourishes.
Joy plumps the branches with
living sap that causes the buds
of fruit to appear,
the fulfillment of its purpose.
The cycle of life,
the abundant life,
operates only within the Vine.

THE RIDE

"You will keep him in perfect peace whose mind is stayed on You because he trusts in You." Isaiah 26:3 (NKJV)

Round and round,
my life has been
like a carnival ride.
Ever faster, more frantic
the turning.
I've loved the spin,
enjoyed the rushing,
the demands,
the thrill of importance.

But now the ride is over.
I am tired; I step out,
dizzy, light-headed,
reaching for support.
God, you're waiting for me...
to cease the spin,
put my feet
upon the ground,
to hold on to You.

The flashing lights of the midway
tug at me still;
I want to ride again.
O, Lord, help me choose a
slower one this time.

A-A-H-H-H!

"He Himself has said, 'I will never leave you nor forsake you." Hebrews 13:5 (NKJV)

I was wondering the other day if I have
really let God say this to me...
How would I behave differently if I allowed
this powerful whisper to dominate my heart?

Perhaps I can liken it to coming home
after a vacation, or time away;
the comfort of our home, our own bed,
our own routine and schedule.
From that relief, contentment floods me.

Realizing that my spirit
is at home with God gives me
—at soul level—that same relief.
In trusting that knowledge, resting on it
as I do on my own pillow,
I place everything on its permanence,
and it brings contentment.
A-a-h-h-h!

And I am learning the truth that
God is at work in my life every moment.
Every conversation, every interruption,
is of Him, and though I may devise a plan for my day,
I must be ready for Him to jump in with another.
I think my tendency is to rush frantically about,
trying to arrive at the place where I already am.
I yearn for the deep rest that complete trust brings,
to feel always the peacefulness of the
first night back in my own bed,
a-a-h-h-h!

SWEET SLEEP

*"I will both lie down in peace, and sleep, for You alone,
O LORD, make me dwell in safety." Psalm 4:8 (NKJV)*

The thought of rest is so appealing.
It evokes a desire in me
to abandon responsibilities, chores and duties
for just a little while; to sleep.

Father, the psalmist says he will both
lie down in peace and sleep.
I guess it's possible to sleep without peace,
but how much more sweet physical sleep is
when my heart is at peace.
My safety, my real rest comes from
trust in You.
Your gift to me as Your beloved,
if I choose to open it,
is peaceful slumber.

Abandoning my works, my self and struggles
to the One Who carried them to the cross,
is the truth of salvation.
Trusting You with my physical cares brings
sleep to my body and mind;
trusting You with my eternity brings rest
to my soul.

How sweet to my spirit are both!

NOT BY SIGHT

"For we walk by faith and not by sight."
2 Corinthians 5:7 (NKJV)

Do I need to have these words
emblazoned across each window,
each mirror, each direction I look?
Because I confess I want to see.
I am anxious to know what awaits...
so I can plan, I guess.

My human nature pokes its nose
into my thoughts and demands satisfaction,
to know what to expect,
and I get frightened when I can't see ahead.

I'm discovering I trust the illusion
that I am in control
rather than the fact of God's sovereignty,
the reality that it is He who rules, not I.

Even though I have flashes of faith,
walking in it is a life-style,
not occasional wind sprints.
It is a steady plodding
along the dusty road of life on earth,
a willing obedience to trust.

So maybe it would be a good idea to paste
the words of this verse wherever I look,
to remind myself that I cannot see,
not really...faith means that I will not...
but I must keep walking anyway.

EROSION

"...and all drank the same spiritual drink, for they drank of that spiritual Rock that followed them: and that Rock was Christ." I Corinthians 10:4 (NKJV)

The canyon walls rise high above,
surrounding me;
streaked by time and
elements into an object
of wonder.

Rock walls, seemingly hard
and impenetrable, worn away
by erosion.
Floods, snow, ice and wind
have worked over time,
changing the appearance of the rock,
altering its form and shape.

I stand in wonder,
gazing at the striated stones,
and think of the rock in the wilderness
from which poured water
to slake the thirst of a multitude,
and praise You, Father, for Your Son,
from Whom living water flows.

He is the Rock upon which my faith stands,
a Rock never alterable by time or elements,
the focus of my worship, changeless forever,
impervious to erosion.

MOSAIC

"The sacrifices of God are a broken spirit,
a broken and a contrite heart—these, O God,
You will not despise." Psalm 51:17 (NJKV)

I would have thought
my life was useless;
all spent on pleasing myself.
But the shards of shattered clay
that I would have kicked aside from the path
have found usefulness in Your hand, my Father;
becoming an object of beauty
You are creating from broken pieces.

A mosaic cannot be made from wholeness,
only from brokenness.
The years of stumbling, running,
selfish pain and fear,
though showing the resultant jagged edges of rebellion,
somehow form a part of the pattern when placed
into a mosaic by the loving hands
of the Master Designer.

Art from rubble; how can it be?
Though far beyond my understanding,
God is able to take whatever I bring
from wherever I've been,
and use it for the mosaic
He's creating with me.

NO GRAVEN IMAGES

"Thou shall not make unto thee any graven image, or any
likeness of any thing that is in heaven above, or that is in
the earth beneath or that is in the water under the earth.
Thou shall not bow down thyself to them, nor serve them:
for I the LORD thy God am a jealous God..."
Exodus 20:4, 5 (KJV)

High above the jungle the ruins rise,
monuments to a past civilization,
marveled upon, exclaimed over,
and visited by millions.
Incredible carvings on stone
impact viewers with a sense of history lived,
of the gods worshiped.
There is wonder expressed in the appreciation
of intricate design and brilliant engineering.

But I have to pause and let my mind reflect
on two tablets of stone I read about in Scripture
upon which were engraved words, the very words
of the One who created the stone,
declaring His Sovereignty, His design,
His demand to be worshiped alone.
Stones, carved by the finger of God,
keep me mindful of His holiness—
the standard I can never meet—
and His mercy that took
the words on those graven stones
and fulfilled them in the flesh of His Son,
the Word Himself.

These high places, these ruins, are not for me.
My faith rests in my Redeemer.

THE POTTER'S HANDS

*"Then I went down to the potter's house, and there he was,
making something at the wheel. And the vessel that he made
of clay was marred in the hand of the potter; so he made it
again into another vessel, as it seemed good to the potter to
make." Jeremiah 18:3-4 (NKJV)*

As a vessel I am useless, Lord,
unless I'm filled with You.
Though I strive with all my might,
my self-willed efforts just won't do.

I pulled away from the Potter's hands,
the work He started put on hold.
I'm chipped and marred, battered, worn
from refusing to let His plan unfold.

The Potter's wheel sits silent; still,
His eager hands are poised above,
waiting for my submissive will
to yield to the molding of His love.

I want to turn back to the Potter,
become a shapeless lump of clay,
and let His hands begin afresh
to form my life to walk His way.

Lord, take my bitter, lonely years;
grind them into dust. Then blend it
gently; mix it with your tender tears
and use that clay as you intended.

continued

I yield now to the Potter's hands,
convinced of His consummate skill.
He made me, so He understands
just how to bend me to His will.

There's joy in resting in those hands,
as I perceive His goal.
He'll spin the wheel, He'll smooth and shape
and I'll be completely mended, whole.

CASTING

"Cast your burden on the Lord and he shall sustain you."
Psalm 55:22 (NKJV)

For so long I have had a misconception.
I'd consider casting my burden on God,
yet somehow that never seemed
to rid me of it.
I thought "casting upon" meant "throwing it at",
thus relieving myself from carrying it.
I don't think that any more.

I'm discovering that God allows burdens,
wants us to carry them sometimes,
but He wants us to ask Him
for His help in doing so;
He desires us to yoke up with Him
and use His shoulder
to share the load.

We must be wise in discerning the burden.
Is it of God for my growth, my strengthening?
Or did I lay it upon myself
from some sense of guilt or responsibility?

continued

As I consider the word "casting"
I can't help but think of a fisherman, fly-casting.
He expertly tosses his hook across the water...
not throwing it to rid himself of it,
but to catch something...a fish!
He still holds the pole, still is part of the process,
but casts his line in hope to receive.
And never does he cast without hope.

When I "cast" my burden on God,
may it be with a sense of hope...
for His strength to bear it.
I think we are not to be care free,
nor careless.
Rather, we are cared for.

POVERTY

"Blessed are the poor in spirit..." Matthew 5:3 (NKJV)

My own poverty.
Have I ever truly realized it?
Always there is the urge to do something
in my own strength and abilities to
make myself more worthy.
Often I say "I can't do it.
I need to rely on Jesus",
but I say it with a sense
of discouraging failure.
That makes it all about me.
What I want is to say,
"I can't do it.
However, I don't have to.
He will. Hallelujah!"

The words are the same;
The difference is huge because
it indicates the condition of my heart.
Instead of a joyful abandon to obedience
God hears only my complaint,
"Oh, dear, I messed up.
I guess I can't do it without Your spirit.
Oh, well, You're going to have to intervene
and haul me out of trouble. Again."

When I look deep inside, I think the
whining voice expresses how I truly feel,
no matter how noble-sounding my words.

Father, forgive me.

BREATH OF LIFE

*"The LORD God formed the man from the dust of the
ground and breathed into his nostrils the breath of life, and
man became a living soul." Genesis 2:7 (NIV)*

A breath; taken without thinking.
Begun at my birth with a tender slap,
it continues until extinguished
by the same Breath that made me
a living soul.
Provided to empower
my physical body to flourish,
the ability to breathe,
how marvelous!

Are faith and trust
as natural for me
as inhaling, exhaling
and processing elements
from earth's atmosphere?
The Source of my physical breath,
the enabling Power for my soul to flourish
longs for my dependence.

Incomplete trust and weak faith
are gasping for air,
merely enough to survive.
And I wonder...
am I inhaling
the oxygen of His presence?
Processing it properly?
Exhaling His peace?
Or am I simply gasping?

HIS LOVE REMAINS

"Hear my cry, O God, listen to my prayer. From the ends of the earth I call to you. I call as my heart grows faint; lead me to the Rock that is higher than I. For you have been my refuge, a strong tower against the foe. I long to dwell in your tent forever and take refuge in the shelter of your wings." Psalm 61:1-4 (NIV)

I'm learning about intimacy,
especially with God.
It's a delightful result of intense focus...
concentration, not on myself,
but on the One I desire.

Changing the focus of my eyes
draws my heart away.
I can sense it happening...
The things of the old life begin
again to have a more definite appeal;
stress and worry increase
and the mantle of selfishness
drapes itself over my shoulders.

Then a word of scripture,
or a verse of song penetrates my mind.
I sense Him whisper my name and
my heart begins to ache with loss.

continued

So I wrench my gaze from myself
to the face of God and let
His tender forgiveness begin
to mend the shattered pieces.

He hasn't moved.
His love remains.

And I am restored, once more,
to the delight of intimacy.

HOPE

"Because I live, you will live too." John 14:19 (HCSB)

The springs of hope
water my soul.
A fountain within me
bubbles incessantly
with the refreshing truth
that life eternal,
in the presence of God,
awaits me.

It is promised.
I believe it.
I drink of its sweetness.
I rest in it.

Hope.

QUIETNESS AND CONFIDENCE

*"For thus says the LORD God, the Holy One of Israel,
'In returning and rest you shall be saved, in quietness and
confidence shall be your strength.' But you would not."
Isaiah 30:15 (NKJV)*

My spirit has been disquieted.
I feel adrift, as though my anchor has lifted.
But in the hurried pace of daily living
I only spend a fleeting moment wondering why.

I don't really have to look far for help...
God speaks plainly through the scripture.
My prayers have been mostly frantic appeals,
panicky pleas, and while I am convinced
that God hears them, I realize I want more.

I want a life-style of faith and trust;
with a knowledge of God that doesn't need
to rush screaming into His presence when
crises occur; a confidence that is
steadfast, unflappable.

Is that not what brings joy
to Your heart, Father?
Your child leaning a little harder,
holding on a bit tighter,
drawing strength
from closeness
with You?

STILLED

"LORD, my heart is not haughty, nor my eyes lofty. Neither do I concern myself with great matters, nor with things too profound for me. Surely I have calmed and quieted my soul, like a weaned child with his mother; like a weaned child is my soul within me." Psalm 131 (NKJV)

I fuss. I fret.
I get concerned over the state of
the world,
my surroundings,
my family.
That is not trust.

I cannot fix the world.
I may be able to affect my surroundings.
I can concern myself with my family.

But things that are too weighty and
awesome for me
must rest from my fretting
while I nestle in the arms of my Father
like I, as a little child,
did with my mother...
and hope in Him.

REPOSE

"The LORD your God is with you, he is mighty to save.
He will take delight in you he will quiet you with his love,
he will rejoice over you with singing."
Zephaniah 3:17 (NIV)

Please still the turbulence in my soul,
dear Father.
The turmoil that rages,
the struggle that stifles,
need not be.
It is your love that brings the calm,
encircling me with all I need for quietness.

In that love I can find safety,
because You are mighty to save.
In that love I can find joy
because you delight in me.
In that love I can find rest
because You are with me.

As I sit before You this morning,
desiring to hear from You,
I read the promises to me in Your word,
and sense the sounds of Your singing.

And my soul finds its repose in You.

Living

"I have been crucified with Christ and I no longer live, but Christ lives in me. The life I live in the body, I live by faith in the Son of God, who loved me and gave himself for me."

Galatians 2:26 (NIV)

SHOES

"Stand firm, then, with the belt of truth buckled around your waist, with the breastplate of righteousness in place, and with your feet fitted with the readiness that comes from the gospel of peace." Ephesians 6:14, 15 (NIV)

Father, I was just thinking…
the kind of shoes I wear
determines how I walk, doesn't it?

If I have my walking shoes on, I stride,
without worrying so much about what is under my foot.
If I wear thin-soled shoes I walk tentatively,
mindful of stones and sharp objects, or water puddles.
With slides or sandals,
I limp slowly…they slip off,
make my ankles turn, cause me to stumble.

Is there a lesson for me here?
I am impatient and don't want to bother
with tying and untying, so I grab the easy ones,
pretty ones that have the chance to trip me or hurt me.
It pleases my vanity and saves me trouble,
but doesn't help my walk.

Father, I need to be sure in my spiritual walk
that I'm taking the time
to lace up my walking shoes,
prepared with the gospel,
or I may stumble because I've taken
the easy way and worn the pretty sandals.

Though You call beautiful the feet of those
who carry the gospel of peace,
to be beautiful in Your eyes, feet must be shod
in sturdy, supporting gospel-laced shoes!

THE FIREPLACE STAGE

"I will sing of the mercies of the LORD forever; with my mouth will I make known Your faithfulness to all generations." Psalm 89:1 (NKJV)

A hearthstone of marble fronts the fireplace
and provides a platform for performing...
when you're four.

Christmas dinner over, the family sinks
into sofas and chair to absorb the bounty;
but this merely provides a captive audience...
when you're four.

Mounting the fireplace stage,
arms extended to embrace us all,
she announces: "Quiet, everybody!
I have a pronouncement to make...
I'm going to sing about Jesus."
Trying to cover up affectionate chuckles, we
observe the performance of this incredibly
talented star (our grandchild)
and hear the Gospel sung in a sweet young voice,
"Jesus loves us so much. Jesus loves us all.
He died for us all. For forgiveness."
On and on the verses come, extemporaneous,
unrehearsed; comical, yet beautiful.

Yes, we laughed...but it was a tender moment.
Joy and pride intermingled, and I thought how
easy to share the wonder of Jesus, with all eyes on you...
when you're four.

When was the last time I stood on the fireplace stage
of my life and sang salvation's song to everyone,
whether or not they wanted to hear?
How beautifully children can teach,
reaching the depths of our hearts,
even when they're four!

WITHERED FRUIT

*"But the fruit of the Spirit is love, joy, peace, patience,
kindness, goodness, faithfulness, gentleness, self-control."
Galatians 5:22, 23 (NIV)*

*"Abide in me and I in you. As the branch cannot
bear fruit of itself, unless it abides in the vine,
neither can you, unless you abide in Me."
John 15:4 (NKJV)*

I took a long look at the fruit I'm bearing, Lord,
this morning when I searched Your word.
And I realized that it is not inviting, tasty, or
good for partaking.

No, peering closely I see
only dry and withered fruit...
pride, envy, impatience, unkindness, frustration.
The place of joining,
the junction of abiding,
has pulled apart and is drying up
without the life-giving sap of the Vine.
It is not a comfortable thought to face.

Father, will you, the Vinedresser,
wrap my branch tight against the Vine again?
Re-graft me into You
so I might feel anew the pulsing flow of
the Vine life;
withered fruit dropping off by Your pruning,
and blossoms of new-forming fruit
beginning to appear.

TOIL

"So why do you worry about clothing? Consider the lilies
of the field, how they grow; they neither toil nor spin and
yet I say to you that even Solomon in all his glory was not
arrayed like one of these. Matthew 6:28, 29 (NKJV)

Why do I toil and spin?
Lilies need not;
and their loveliness delights the eye.
From bulbs in the earth,
to green sprigs, then regal bloom
they *do* nothing...they just *are*.

All that is necessary is in the seed,
planted by the gardener,
watered by the rain.

I guess I needn't worry, Father,
about my beauty
when you've promised
to clothe me with your loveliness.

It's all there in the bulb inside me,
waiting to bloom.
Planted by your Spirit,
watered by your Son's sacrificial blood;
I don't have to work for it,
I just have to be...
Your child.

YARDSTICK

"...do not rejoice that the spirits submit to you, but rejoice that your names are written in heaven." Luke 10:20 (NIV)

"Am I now trying to win the approval of men, or of God?" Galatians 1:10a (NIV)

I find myself measuring tonight,
adding up the good deeds,
examining them
against the yardstick of success
that I use to establish my worth.

As night falls and my head rests
on the softness of my pillow
I contemplate the activity
that defines my days and I wonder,
"How did I do?"

Perhaps, though, I should use
a different yardstick.
Perhaps I should ask my Maker...
"Did I grow today?
Did I draw nearer to You?
Am I more like You?"

I think I should use a yardstick
that measures distance rather than height;
one that will show how near I am to God
rather than how high the
pile of good deeds.

Because, after all, that's how You
measure my life, isn't it, Father?

MARGINS

"There was not a word of all that Moses had commanded
that Joshua did not read to the whole assembly of Israel
including the women and children, and the aliens who lived
among them." Joshua 8:35 (NIV)

I meticulously set the margins
in the document I'm creating;
careful to make sure that the finished product
will be neat and tidy.
There's an adjustment I can make,
a button to push; it's easy.
So easy, in fact, that I wonder
if perhaps I use the same tactic in my life.
Anything that might be messy,
or destroy the beauty and symmetry of
my carefully constructed self,
people who might be outside my margins,
are rearranged, and thus ignored,
by a push of a button in my heart.

In my stubborn insistence to keep
the margins set, I am pushing aside
the whisper of God...the Creator,
the God Whose heart bleeds for His creation...
Who sets no margins against those
who may be aliens within my narrow world,
and pleads for me to do the same.

THE BUILDER

"By the grace God has given me, I laid a foundation as an
expert builder, and someone else is building on it. But each
one should be careful how he builds. For no one can lay
any foundation other than the one already laid, which is
Jesus Christ." I Corinthians 3:10-11 (NIV)

An old house sits neglected, derelict.
Dead weeds shroud its sidewalk,
vines creep through shattered windows,
and sagging doors give way only to curious wildlife.
I pass it often; it is an unwelcome eyesore.
"Tear it down. It's ugly," people say.

But one day a builder comes.
Seeing past the dilapidated exterior,
he begins to strip away all that is broken,
and old, and ugly.
I am astonished to watch how
the new structure rises from the old foundation
and I think that is what you did for me, God,
when I finally bowed my knee.

The foundation was laid in my heart long ago.
Stripping away the ugly pride
and rebellion that made me unusable,
You attached new wood, new paint,
new shingles, making the building
of my life a worthy structure,
recycled by a Builder Who sees value
in what many would tear down and discard.

God, there are so many derelict lives
in this world; existing with
shattered dreams and shrouded hopes.
You are the builder;
You see the value in each one.
May I never pass by a broken life
without seeing with Your eyes,
and letting You use me
as a builder's apprentice.

FREEZE FRAME

"But the father said to his servants, 'Quick! Bring the best robe and put it on him. Put a ring on his finger and sandals on his feet. Bring the fattened calf and kill it. Let's have a feast and celebrate. For this son of mine was dead and is alive again; he was lost and is found.'"
Luke 15:22-24 (NIV)

It was like a movie on a screen;
the story of the prodigal son playing in my mind.
Each emotion pictured on the face of the son
was mirrored in my heart and I know I'm the prodigal.
"I must return," I'd said.
Desiccated husks of sin no more appealed.
Arid loneliness and a thirst for peace,
for belonging, filled my empty soul.
All my resources gone,
I turned my face toward home.

And now here I am, clasped in my Father's arms.

The story plays on, the prodigal son is invited
to join the party wearing the new robe
provided by his exuberant father.
Then comes a freeze frame
and I suddenly realize I'm caught there.
It is good to be home, but unwilling
to don the new robe, I stand outside the door,
insisting upon my unworthiness.
There's food to eat, and a ready welcome
but I have been rejecting the celebration,
refusing the new robe,
struggling with deeds to prove I am worthy.
The freeze frame convicts.

I need forgiveness, again.
My Father waits patiently for me
to abandon my work and let Him
wrap His mercy around my shoulders
and welcome me to the fullness of joy.

Let the camera roll.
I just realized
I'm the honored guest at a banquet!

BEHIND THE FOOTLIGHTS

"Trust in the LORD with all your heart; and lean not on your own understanding. In all your ways acknowledge him and he shall direct your paths". Proverbs 3:5 & 6 (NKJV)

Trusting God's guidance, His direction,
is rather like being an actor in a play.
The script is written.
God is Author, Producer, Director.
I signed the contract at salvation,
agreeing to follow the instructions
of the director and producer.
How disruptive and arrogant
it is for me to step to the front of the stage and say
"I think my part would be better if I…"!
But that's what I have insisted upon doing
so many times.
Instead of learning from Him I keep trying
to adapt the role to fit myself.
So I am waiting in the wings,
ready for the first step to the stage, again.
I have determined to continue the role
God has designed for me,
that of a disciple,
and the curtain is about to rise anew
on this very real portrayal in my life.

I must become more familiar with the script
and follow the Director more closely.
It is on His shoulders, after all,
that the ultimate success of
the production rests.

BALANCE

"Martha, Martha," the Lord answered, "you are worried
and upset about many things, but only one thing is needed.
Mary has chosen what is better, and it will not be taken
away from her." Luke 10:41, 42 (NIV)

Teetering down the sidewalk,
my grandson bravely navigates his
adventurous first trip on his two-wheeler...
without training wheels!!
Head bobbing from right to left,
eyes scrunched tight in concentration
he struggles, intent on keeping his balance.

I watch him, and observe, too,
his daddy running along beside,
encouraging, instructing, ready to catch him,
should he tip too far to one side
and lose that precarious balance.

And it brought a picture to my mind
of my own struggles.
Riding the two-wheeler of my responsibilities
and commitments, I am striving to find balance,
careful not to lean too far in either direction.
Too many duties, or too few?
Too much relaxation or not enough?
I am learning a lesson today,
as I watch this little child;
discovering that balance is vital
in keeping upright, moving ahead,
and not tipping over.

continued

But the most beautiful thing I see
is my heavenly Father running
along beside me, encouraging, instructing,
and sweetly waiting to catch me if I lean
too far to either side.
Speaking His word,
the truth of His love and care for me,
into my heart, He restores my balance.
I've used my training wheels long enough, I think.
I need only keep my eyes on Him
to ride straight and true.

ON TIPTOE

"Walk in wisdom toward those who are outside,
redeeming the time. Let your speech always be with grace,
seasoned with salt, that you may know how you ought
to answer each one." Colossians 4:5-6 (NKJV)

Somehow I had the picture of
successful Christianity as
seasoned warriors striding forth waving
the Sword as a banner.
But here I read that we are to walk
in wisdom, and I am thinking
that stomping out to the battleground
may not be the best plan.
What if in my stomping I crush
something, or somebody, fragile?
Or isn't it more than possible to step
into something messy or dirty?
Or to march so loudly I am unable
to hear the voice of my Commander?

continued

No, I think perhaps walking on tiptoe
is more what God has in mind.
Carefully, circumspectly, cautiously,
watchful with wisdom from above,
yet confidently forward...
sort of as a child coming downstairs
on Christmas morning.
Quietly determined, expectant,
prepared for something extraordinary.
Hesitant, careful only in order
not to disturb the ecstasy of the moment.
Gifts await.

If we walk on tiptoe,
cautious where we step,
gracefully obedient,
the gifts from above
will never disappoint.

THE HANDS OF A FATHER

*"He tends His flock like a shepherd; He gathers the lambs
in his arms and carries them close to his heart; he gently
leads those that have young." Isaiah 40:11 (NIV)*

I was watching a family today,
father, mother, children,
as they walked along the street.
The youngest child,
just learning to walk with tiny, stumbling steps,
would never have been able to keep up
with the rest of the family had not
his daddy slowed his own steps,
leaned down to clasp the hand of his son
and chided the older children not to
skip ahead, to wait for him.

I began to watch the crowd
a bit more closely as it passed by.
It was easy to distinguish an adult
walking with a small child
by the slow measured pace and
slanting of the body to accommodate
short legs and small steps.

continued

In a strange way I was moved to tears
as I considered how sweetly it reminded
me of the heavenly Father.
When we first begin our walk
within the family of God, our steps are small,
our legs of faith short and stumbling.
But God leans down, grips our hand and
with sweet encouragement measures
His pace to ours.

Yes, some of us have stronger legs and
we try to run ahead of Him;
but He reminds us to wait;
that He is in control and His plan will allow
all of us in the family to arrive together.

Whatever the pace we walk within the family,
how precious to remember
we are kept in a circle of care
that is surrounded by
the hands of our Father.

THE PARADE

*"Since we live by the Spirit, let us keep in step with the
Spirit." Galatians 5:25 (NIV)*

It's the beginning of a new year,
and I watched the Rose Parade today.
The intricately beautiful floats,
unbelievably imaginative,
the cheering crowds
and commentator's voice-overs
with explanations of each flower and seed
applied to create such marvels of design.

But what truly thrills me are the bands;
marching in precision,
in perfect unity to the beat of the drums,
following their leaders.
I love to watch their feet and remembering
from my own band experiences,
how difficult it is to keep in step, I admire them.
And as I watch I realize
that if everyone would walk along
without heeding the rhythm
there would be no point in watching them.

So when I read this verse, it occurs to me
that the same thing must be true
of followers of Jesus.
If we all marched to the rhythm of the Spirit
not only would our music be a delight to hear,
but our unity would draw attention
and enthrall the watching world.

SHIFTING GEARS

"...as for me, being on the way, the Lord led me..."
Genesis 24:27 (NKJV)

Asking for God's leading has become
a habit in my life;
a comfortable part of a daily routine
that is my answer to what I *should* do.

But I read His Word and
it convicted my heart...
One small phrase,
"being on the way, the Lord led me...",
and I wonder, am I on the way, moving?
Or am I stuck in Neutral, or even worse,
in Park?

Is it time to shift gears
and begin to move?
I am held back by my fears
of going the wrong direction.
Am I willing to trust that
"being on the way"
will bring me to the place
to which He is leading me?
Or will I just sit here in
the parking lot?

LEFTOVER GRACE

"We then, as workers together with Him also plead with
you not to receive the grace of God in vain."
2 Corinthians. 6:1 (NKJV)

Leftover grace.
Is there such a thing?
Perhaps it's sort of like the manna
God provided in the wilderness.
The Israelites were told to take enough for one day;
only for the Sabbath were they to take any extra.
Leftover manna spoiled, turned rotten,
useful only for the time it was needed.

Grace, a miracle, like manna,
supplied from a loving God, is under His control.
Just as there was always enough manna for the day,
there is always grace enough
for every moment of need.

I'm wondering, though, if I'm not operating under
the assumption of grace;
knowing it's there and available
but more as a covering for what I have done,
rather than an ever-fresh,
moment-by-moment supply,
a running faucet from which to fill my cup
regularly and often.

Living "under grace" means gathering it
for present immediacy, instead of relying
on grace left over from yesterday's troubles;
dwelling, moving and operating in the
midst of a constantly flowing river of grace.

THE NEW HOUSE

"Therefore if anyone is in Christ, he is a new creation; the old has gone, the new has come!" 2 Corinthians 5:17 (NIV)

God, You have blessed us
with a new house.
So clean, pristine, in its newness,
a delight to my senses.
Smelling like fresh paint,
everything gleaming,
no marks anywhere;
it is wonderful just walking
in the door.

I long for lovely things to fill it.
Somehow my old shabby furniture
doesn't seem to fit there.

Father, I was thinking the other day,
You have blessed me with a new heart.
Do you feel as I do when I look at my
new house, so clean and unmarked,
and know the old shabby sinfulness
doesn't seem to fit anymore?
You long to replace it with lovely new things,
but I keep dragging the old comfortable stuff
back into it, even as I decry its shabbiness.

Dear Father, will you help me
see my fresh new heart as You do...
as I see my new house...
and understand that my old ugly sin
has no place there;
that when You clean me up, You only desire
to put beautiful new furnishings in the
great room of my heart,
where You have taken up residence.

STALKS OF FLAX

"(But she had taken them up to the roof and hidden them under the stalks of flax she had laid out on the roof.)"
Joshua 2:6 (NIV)

Two spies,
under stalks of flax,
hidden in God's mercy
by a chance encounter.

Was it chance?
No. It never is with God.
Unlikely? Yes.
But the prior preparation...
a softened heart,
an open door
and a rooftop refuge...
was God at work beneath
a surface that breathed
enmity toward Him.

Am I hiding under
stalks of flax,
reveling in His merciful covering?
Just doing my job,
spying out the land.

Or am I under the stalks of flax
waiting, ready when I hear the words,
"Get up and go",
fully involved in the work He's doing?

I want to be. I want to see.
I want to be alert
to hear and follow as He leads.

Just what *am* I doing
under these
stalks of flax?

HIND'S FEET IN LOW PLACES

*"The Sovereign Lord is my strength; he makes my feet like
the feet of a deer, he enables me to go on the heights."
Habakkuk 3:19 (NIV)*

We have spent the summer entertaining
a family of deer where we live.
A doe and her two young ones have
felt very comfortable munching on
our fallen apples and budding roses.
It has been an experience to watch them.

I read this verse in scripture, however,
and think of our friendly forest guests;
how delicately they walk upon the flatlands.
Mincing steps and cautious tread carry
them along until they are startled by an
unfamiliar sound or perceived threat.
Then they bound with great leaps up the
hills and into deep woods where safety beckons.
Their feet are made for this, for the hills;
not for the flat, even ground.
They are at their created best,
climbing and jumping, though often they
must come down among us for food to survive.

And so I was thinking about my own feet,
created to be leaping upon the high hills
of fellowship with my God.
He made my feet, not to scrabble for
survival on the flatland of earth,
to limp along its hot pavement,
but to climb to the safety of His presence;
to the deep woods of His protection.
Instead I mince along with little steps,
scrabbling, eating whatever I can find.

Father, please startle me with the scent of danger
from the enemy of my soul,
so I can use my feet as You made them to be...
running with no thought of what is underfoot,
to You on Your high hills.

REARRANGED

*"Make me hear joy and gladness, that the bones you have
broken may rejoice...Create in me a clean heart, O God,
and renew a steadfast spirit within me."*
Psalm 51:8, 10 (NKJV)

Injury;
a joint out of place.
unbelievable pain,
uselessness.
Experts pull, press,
restore the shoulder.
Relief indescribable follows
the agony of correction.

A dislocated heart—
out of joint with God.
How the pain of separation
immobilizes.
But the Great Physician
can press and pull
and restore a dislocated soul.

Sometimes hurt comes
from the injury,
sometimes from the fixing;
always, though, there
follows relief
when all is back in place.

WILLINGNESS

"...and I will very gladly spend and be spent for your souls..." 2 Corinthians 12:15 (NKJV)

Broken bread,
poured-out wine.
A life given to others
for love of Jesus.
How high and noble,
how spiritual, it sounds as I say it.
But is it true, God?
You see my heart.
Am I honestly willing to be broken?
Am I truly seeking to be poured out?
To thank You for the stunning gift
of my salvation, I want to be.

Yet even as I mouth the words of surrender
I find the cork still
deeply embedded in my bottle
and the crust of my loaf seems resistant to breaking.
I seem perfectly willing only to drip,
and toss a few stray crumbs of bread.

It's all about willingness,
isn't it, Lord?
Mine, as opposed to Yours.
You were willing to be broken for me.
Where is my willingness to be broken
and poured out for You?

Dare I say I want to be willing?

FLUTTERING

*"The LORD is good to those whose hope is in him, to
the one who seeks him; it is good to wait quietly for the
salvation of the LORD." Lamentations 3:25, 26 (NIV)*

I prayed this morning, Father,
and asked you to direct my day.
I would just be still and trust You.

But I wonder, as I lie here
struggling to find quietness,
if I am really still.
My intention is to be so,
yet I sense myself fluttering,
much as a tiny bird itching to fly.

Pulled by the breezes of responsibilities
I am reluctant to cease my motion
but I need to learn...
the strength to fly comes
only from lying perfectly still
in the palm of Your hand.

Loving

"Love the Lord your God with all your heart and all your soul and with all your strength and with all your mind. And love your neighbor as yourself."

Luke 10:27 (NIV)

ALWAYS, IN ALL WAYS

*"The LORD appeared to us in the past, saying, 'I have
loved you with an everlasting love. I have drawn you with
loving-kindness.'" Jeremiah 31:3 (NIV)*

I opened a faded envelope today,
its contents torn and worn from many readings.
All I have left of my father, of his person,
are these few letters penned after I had left home,
rebellious, running,
my face turned to my imagined freedom,
my back to the rules.

So I take these precious scraps of paper,
letting my eyes alight on his final words to me
"I love you always, in all ways, Daddy".

I weep to think he never knew that I returned,
repentant,
and found my Heavenly Father's arms opened wide;
His beloved words
"I love you always, in all ways"
signed in the blood drops of His Son
on His letter of reconciliation to me.

TEARS

*"I am weary with my groaning; all night I make my bed
swim; I drench my couch with my tears. My eye wastes
away because of grief...the LORD has heard the voice of
my weeping. The LORD has heard my supplication; the
LORD will receive my prayer." Psalm 6:6-9 (NKJV)*

Deep in my being
there is an ocean of tears.
It comes unbidden,
unexpected, unwelcome.
Like the tide it flows in,
piling up the driftwood of remembrance
and leaving the debris of pain behind
as it rolls back and forth in my heart.

Here on the shore
I'm lost in the logjam;
tears freshening with each thought,
recollection, old memory...
reliving hurt, searching for peace.
I am learning, however, that those tears
are meant to wash away
the refuse that clogs my soul.
It is my heavenly Father's cleansing.
He washes my heart, as tears wash my eyes,
so that I can see Him more clearly.

Will I ever cease to weep, I wonder?

And I think that perhaps I never
want to reach the place
where tears are stopped from flowing
for then I will be hardened...
unresponsive, unfeeling.

Let me keep my tears, Father,
so that I will be cleansed
by Your presence within me,
learning to trust,
learning to flow with the tide that frees me
to love and accept You...
until the day you dry them all
forever.

UMBRELLA

*"Like an apple tree among the trees of the forest is my lover
among the young men. I delight to sit in his shade, and his
fruit is sweet to my taste. He has taken me to the banquet
hall, and his banner over me is love."*
Song of Solomon 2:2-4 (NIV)

Walking along the beach at midnight,
the ocean gently laps the sand beneath my feet,
a cool breeze scents the air; I pause.

Sleep eludes me and the moon
has called me from our rumpled bed.
It's not restlessness I feel, not now,
but a longing to express my joy.

Silver streaks caress the surface,
rolling gently with the ride.
I reflect upon our life; the years spent side by side;
as moments ago I lay in your arms, thanking God
for the comfort He provides for me by giving me you.

We are no longer young. Yet how gloriously sweet,
as heads turn gray and skin once firm begins to droop,
to feel the tingle of excitement, knowing that back there
you are tossing, turning, reaching out for me.

By the time my middle years arrived,
I thought I'd settle into the humdrum; to create a groove
through which my life would smoothly glide.
Peaks and valleys would subside, and I would move
between the boundaries like the sea.

I did not expect this thrill each day...
the fluttering expectance, the delight of being together.
I thought it would fade; this completeness
of joining heart, mind and body before God.

Now I know that love is contentment and sharing
mixed with flashes of joy.
As moonlight polishes the sea, the patina of time together
brings a lightness of heart that comes
from releasing my burden to the umbrella of your care.

MY MOTHER'S PRAYER

"I will open my mouth in parables…so the next generation would know them, even the children yet to be born; and they in turn would tell their children. Then they would put their trust in God, and not forget his deeds, but would keep his commands:" Psalm 78: 2, 6-7 (NIV)

Father, for so long I resented
my motherlessness,
the tearing out of my heart at her death,
the open wound that continues to this day.
Fearing to voice the anger and bitterness
toward You, I acted it out in rebellion, in deceit,
burying my grief.
I didn't want to trust You, Father,
but I believed You, and feared the consequences
of outright disobedience.
So my wrath simmered,
covered with a lid of good works.

But You knew.
You pursued me in my pain,
answering my mother's dying prayer.
I feel her prayers, Father, even now.
Transcending space and time,
they continue to touch my life,
because she entrusted my soul to You.

Thus You prepared a husband for me,
knew my children long before they took a breath,
and designed grandchildren to delight my heart.

I will never on this earth understand, Father,
why You took her to heaven when I needed her so.
Someday I will,
but I trust You now, and I long to see her again,
to join in unceasing praise,
wrapped together in Your love.

BEDROCK

"And you shall know the truth and the truth shall make you free." John 8:32 (NKJV)

Bedrock, solid rock beneath
the soil and superficial stones,
a foundation.
God's bedrock is truth,
and He calls me to stand upon it,
to know it, to walk in it.

But I think, in our society today,
truth is sort of a misty concept,
becoming fuzzy and fudged, and,
I have to admit, easy to ignore.

Jesus said knowing the truth
would set me free.
Maybe the fact that I sometimes
feel bound and stifled is that the chains
are of my own making;
that I have indulged in some deceitful behavior,
some dishonesty, not told the whole truth,
not walked entirely upright,
excusing myself because it seemed
just a little deviation, a small sidestep.

I do want to be free.

What is the truth that I need to know?
It is that I am loved.
Loved by the God of the Universe...
my Creator, Who IS truth.
When that fact becomes burned
into my brain, into the very core of me,
there comes a freedom to live, to love;
a willingness to trust,
a longing to walk with the One Who
holds my hand and will never let it go.

And everything else falls into place.

TRANSPLANT

*"This is love, not that we loved God, but that He loved us,
and sent His Son as an atoning sacrifice for our sins."*
I John 4:10 (NIV)

Love is not native to the soil
of the human heart.
Not the kind of love God has for us,
for all mankind.
We talk about it, sing about it, think about it,
but aside from a renewed, transformed heart
the kind of love we need to adore God
and love our neighbors cannot exist.
It must be a transplant,
carried by the Holy Spirit into the
heart of man from the heart of God.

And once transplanted,
though even at its highest and best,
human love falls far below the wonder
of the glory of God's love.

Often, an exotic plant,
though not indigenous to its new home,
can flourish with the proper care and nurture.
So it is with us. We cannot grow love.
We can only prepare the soil of our hearts
to receive it, and let it bloom within,
and spread to others,
by the power of the love of God,
transplanted.

SIGNATURE

"For we are God's workmanship, created in Christ Jesus
to do good works, which God prepared in advance for us to
do." Ephesians 2:10 (NIV)

Observing an artist the other day,
I was thinking of my life as a painting.
You, Father, saw the finished product in
Your mind's eye before
You ever set the canvas of my days
upon Your easel.

I watch the artist paint;
first sketching the design, the vision,
applying the first layer,
then another and another.
Sometimes, at first,
it doesn't look like much,
the colors muddied, the design unclear,
but the process goes on and,
little by little, the picture emerges.
I begin to see how the dark colors
underneath give the depth and basis for
the highlighting that only the artist
can apply to create the totality of his vision.
And then, upon completion, with a flourish,
he places his signature in the corner
identifying it as his.

continued

Heart Chords

It's not finished yet, the painting of my life,
but one day God will say "Ah, yes, it is done."
And He will put His signature of satisfaction
in the corner,
well pleased with His work
as I carry the beauty of His artistry
into His presence, bringing Him glory
in endless praise.

144

GIDDY-UP

*"For I am convinced that neither death nor life, neither
angels nor demons, neither the present nor the future, nor
any powers, neither height nor depth, nor anything else
in all creation, will be able to separate us from the love of
God that is in Christ Jesus our Lord."*
Romans 8:38-39 (NIV)

You chose, Father, to love us,
this fallen human race.
How gloriously wonderful is that thought!
I sit and wonder how anyone could spit
in the face of such an immense love,
but I do it.

Even though I've asked You
to be my partner, to ride with me,
I leap astride my prancing steed,
grab the reins of my life, settle into the
saddle and say "Giddy-up".
And when I'm thrown from my horse
(which happens with regularity)
I reach up from the mud and expect
a hand from You.
Of course You always extend it;
You keep Your promises, but how
many times do I need to get dumped
before I realize that when two are on
a horse, one must ride behind,
and that one must be me, not You.
You must hold the reins.
It'll be much better if I grab on toYou
than try and manage that horse by myself!

SILENCE

"He was oppressed and afflicted, yet he did not open his mouth; he was led like a lamb to the slaughter, and as a sheep before its shearers is silent, so he did not open his mouth." Isaiah 53:7 (NIV)

It's what You didn't say, Jesus,
on that terrible day
that moves me so.
The eternal Word, silent.
How could You have sustained such agony
without screaming "Stop"?

Knowing Who You are,
knowing Your own power,
knowing the sinfulness of Your tormentors...

That's why, isn't it?
Because of their sinfulness,
and mine.
Your creation spitting at You,
whipping and taunting You...
You didn't say anything.
Knowing You were the only way
of restoration, You participated
in Your beating
by your submission to the torture,
loving with unfathomable grace;
in Your silence
saying everything.

THE MOB

"We have found the Messiah" (that is, the Christ).
And he brought him to Jesus." John 1:41 (NIV)

"With one voice they cried out 'Away with this man!
Release Barabbas to us!' Wanting to release Jesus,
Pilate appealed to them again. But they kept shouting,
'Crucify him, crucify him.'" Luke 23:18, 20-21(NIV)

They followed You, Jesus, for a while.
They thought You were their deliverer.
But it doesn't take much for a mob to turn,
and it turned against You.
despising, rejecting You.

I watched the ugly violence in the faces of the crowd
as the Truth was cast down into the mud made
by His own blood in the dirt.
And I wept with fury against the mob.

But oh, no, when I look closely, I see my own
ugly sin in the sneering visages that fill the screen.
Do I cry "Crucify Him!" with my own refusal to trust?
Do I not kick sand in His bleeding face
over and over again when I esteem too lightly
His choice to die for me?

continued

Please, Lord, burn these images into my brain.
Give me courage to stand against
the Satan-led mob refusing to believe,
and accept my simple Thank You,
though it seems trite to whisper such small words
given the enormity of Your sacrifice.

Yet I long for the sweetness
of Your forgiving gaze washing over me,
cleansing from my countenance
the image of the mob,
restoring to me a trusting face aglow
with gratitude and joy and love.

SWEET SPICES

*"And when the Sabbath was past, Mary Magdalene,
and Mary the mother of James, and Salome, had brought
sweet spices that they might come and anoint Him."
Mark 16:1 (KJV)*

How many times I've read the story
of the resurrection morning!
But somehow now I am struck by the fact
that these women, loving disciples of Jesus,
were bringing sweet spices to cover
the stench of death.
A sorrowful procession,
completely unaware that He was not there.
Long before they had gathered their packets
of pungent herbs and begun their bitter trek
to perform one last act of love,
Jesus had shed His battered body and
exploded in triumph from the dark tomb.
They didn't know, not yet.

And I, wondering if I truly comprehend the power
of the Resurrection, trudge up the garden path
carrying my own sweet spices,
the carefully prepared good deeds,
my efforts to *do* something nice for Jesus.
Should not I be running to the empty tomb
with great freedom and joy, flinging the
sweet spices of His fragrance everywhere,
relying on His mighty power;
the power that has freed me and forgiven me,
to carry His precious aroma,
the pleasing spicy scent of His love,
wherever He sends me?

Lauding

"Praise the LORD.
Praise the LORD, O my soul.
I will praise the LORD with
all my life; I will sing praise to
my God as long as I live."

Psalm 146:1, 2 (NIV)

WORDS

"and the Word became flesh and dwelt among us, and we beheld His glory, the glory as of the only begotten of the Father, full of grace and truth." John 1:14 (NKJV)

I wanted to praise God.
I thought of all His might
and power
and love
and grace
and tried to write it down.

Thwarted by my imperfect pen,
I cried out to Him,
"There are no words…
no words sufficient
to describe You!"

"Oh, yes," He whispered.
"There is – one Word."

NIGHT SONG

*"The Lord will send His faithful love by day, His song will
be with me in the night—a prayer to the God of my life."
Psalm 42:8 (HCSB)*

Sometimes, in the dark stillness
after midnight, I will waken with a song
of praise playing in my ear.
I wonder, when I hear a snippet of a hymn
strummed in my heart or words of worship
pouring through my mind,
what God has just done in me.
Because He must have spoken,
or I wouldn't be so filled with His presence.

Perhaps He's unsnarled
a tangled skein of concern...
or shown my heart a new concept
of Himself that my conscious mind
could not conceive.
Yet, deep at the core of my being
He's revealed His heart to me
and I am restored and awash in His love.

That love carries me in the daytime
when I am awake and responding
on a cognizant level;
but with the night song,
His tender lullaby wraps my soul in joy.

I lift my prayer of praise to You, Father,
sing on!

TRANSCENDENT INTIMACY

*"I will give you a new heart and put a new spirit within
you. I will put My Spirit within you and cause you to walk
in My statutes." Ezekiel 36:26a, 27 (NKJV)*

Transcendence. Intimacy.
It is an oxymoron, a contradiction in terms.
Father, You are the oxymoron's epitome.
How can it be that You, the God of all time,
transcendent above all,
are willing to insert Your sovereign self into
my very heart,
because you desire intimacy with me?

It is completely
beyond my comprehension.
I can do no more than bow
in joyous praise,
allowing the
inconceivable,
the unimaginable,
to descend into reality
and infuse my entire being
with You.

QUIETUDE

"Be still and know that I am God." Psalm 46:10 (KJV)

The hush of
a snowfall,
muffling sound,
brings to my mind
a holy sign.
The God of all creation
sprinkles down
His love
like snowflakes
and begs me for my stillness
so that I will know...
He is God.

COALS ON MY LIPS

"Then one of the seraphs flew to me with a live coal in his hand, which he had taken with tongs from the altar. With it he touched my mouth and said, 'See, this has touched your lips; your guilt is taken away and your sin atoned for."
Isaiah 6:6-7 (NIV)

I hear your voice cry out, O Lord.
I shiver with the thrill of holy call...
The thundering plea resounds,
"Who will go for me?"

Awed, I whisper, "Lord, is it I?
Surely I can't speak your word."
"Yes," He tells me, "go.
I have made you whole.
To you I have dealt my power,
my strength can be your own."

"Then," I cried, "from your altar send
a burning coal to cleanse my lips
as though with fire...
purging, purifying flame,
so that from within my soul
the words are forged and uttered true
through lips alight with hallowed embers,
pure, and sacrificed to you."

INFUSION

"For it is God who works in you, to will and to act
according to his good purpose."
Philippians 2:13 (NIV)

Life.
All is encompassed in that word...
the essence of my soul.

Life.
The source that holds my past
inhabits my present,
shapes my everlasting tomorrows.

Life eternal, in the person of God
the Holy Spirit, is working within me.

My imagination, long having considered
Him as simply a tightly coiled Presence
waiting to spring into action at my nod,
is fired by a new realization
of a living, breathing force
that infuses every cell of my
spiritual being; a pushing, throbbing mist of
LIFE!
Within me. Surrounding me. Inhabiting me.

My mind can scarcely absorb
what my spirit already comprehends...
the presence of vitality, the essence of life...
God Almighty.

WARMTH

*"The LORD bless you and keep you; the LORD
make his face shine upon you and be gracious unto you;
the LORD turn his face toward you and give you peace."
Numbers 6:24-26 (NIV)*

Father, I thank you this morning…
for the first sip of hot coffee;
the cuddly fleece of my robe
and the steamy needling spray
of the shower…
for the warmth of this house
that surrounds me and
reminds me of your care.

But all of these, Father,
are wrapped up
in the warmth of the blessing
as I realize you make your face
to shine upon me.

WIND

"The wind blows to the south and turns to the north;
round and round it goes, ever returning on its course."
Ecclesiastes 1:6 (NIV)

Invisible power,
wild freedom...
going where it wishes,
its presence detected only
by its effects.

Who has not felt the wind?
Who has not suffered its bite?
Or welcomed its cooling breath?

Such a strange phenomenon...
coming from nowhere,
going who knows where.

God's exhalation, perhaps,
blowing through His creation,
gentle, strong, mighty, refreshing,
much as He is Himself;
wafting His character
unseen, ever present, unchangeable.

I never hear or feel the wind
without an accompanying thrill of worship,
giving glory to the Power behind it.

THE EVENING SACRIFICE

"O Lord, I call to you; come quickly to me. Hear my voice when I call to you. May my prayer be set before you like incense; may the lifting up of my hands be like the evening sacrifice." Psalm 141:1-2 (NIV)

What is the evening sacrifice?
Some scholars say it points to Jesus,
offered in the evening of the world,
the final sacrifice, after all the
observances required by the Law;
as atonement for us, that we might
freely exalt God with our lips,
our voices, our prayers.

It is evening now, and I am coming
to offer You my sacrifice of praise...
for Jesus, who Himself was the evening sacrifice;
after the Law, fulfilling the Law,
making it possible for me to cease
from my labors and rest in Him.

continued

May my prayer, my sacrifice of praise,
rise to You to gladden Your heart
with the fragrance of incense.
But just as the aroma of incense
is not released without heat or fire,
my prayer does not ascend
without the holy fire of Your Spirit.

So as I look back over my day,
I consider the heat of the trials that bring me to
the burning of my will, my daily sacrifice;
and realize that through those battling fires
comes the peace that uplifts my hands in praise,
my evening sacrifice.

EXUBERANCE

*"Praise the LORD from the heavens, praise him in the
heights above. Praise him, all his angels, praise him, all
his heavenly hosts. Praise him sun and moon, praise him,
all you shining stars. Praise him, you highest heavens and
you waters above the skies. Let them praise the name of the
LORD, for he commanded and they were created.*
Psalm 148:1-5 (NIV)

*"Let everything that has breath praise the LORD. Praise
the LORD" Psalm 150:6 (NKJV)*

I'm drinking in the beauty,
absorbing it
through every pore of my soul;
scene after scene...
towering pine-crusted mountains,
sparkling, rippling streams
and, stretched above it all,
the azure Montana sky.

With Beethoven on the car stereo,
I'm hurtling along a curving gray ribbon
of highway, my journey taking me home.
Here is where I was born.
This is the loveliness, the staggering grandeur
that infused my childhood;
and, insignificant as I feel beneath
these majestic mountains,
I can feel a stretching,
an expanding inside that delivers me
to their verdant embrace.
I raise my hands, exuberant...
creature and creation joined in worship
of the Creator.

MOUNTAINTOP

"Behold I will create new heavens and a new earth...The
wolf and the lamb will feed together, and the lion will eat
straw like the ox, but dust will be the serpent's food.
They will neither harm nor destroy on all my holy
mountain, says the LORD." Isaiah 65:17a, 25 (NIV)

Picking her way daintily over the hillside,
the doe forages for a few bites of food
and a sip from the pond.
I know she sees me sitting there;
she looks straight at me, but instead of
skittering away in fright,
she bends her legs and lowers herself
to the ground, nestling under the tree beside me.

I am almost afraid to move,
even though I sense her acceptance,
so I sit, motionless, enjoying the scampering
chipmunks and fluttering hummingbirds.
Soon the doe's mate moves majestically into
the clearing, crowned in velvet.
I feel as though I've been privileged to
participate in a real-life scene from "Bambi"!

Peace settles on my shoulders
with the sun's warmth and my heart quiets,
making way for the sounds of softly flowing water
and the sighing of breeze-stirred pines.

Father, I feel honored to be allowed this small glimpse
of the way I think it will be when Your kingdom,
the peaceable kingdom,
inhabits the new earth...
All of your creatures—lion and lamb—
man and forest friends—in unity and harmony,
the way you designed it to be.

The doe looks at me again,
twitches her ears and lowers her head for a nap.
The water continues its trickling flow,
as the young buck finds his own resting place
and I lean back in wonder,
stilled into tranquility,
worshiping.

ALLELUIA!

*"I will praise the LORD all my life; I will sing praise
to my God as long as I live." Psalm 146:2 (NIV)*

Oh, God, my Father, the music...
I am wrapped in beauty!
Surrounded by the hush of holiness
Your whisper fills my depths and
joy begins to rise in chorded cadence
'til harmony erupts in
"Alleluias".

My voice can never match
the euphony in my heart,
nor can my pen express the
adoration of You that
this hymn of praise evokes
in the center of my soul.
Alleluia!

Printed in the United States
218601BV00001B/2/P